MAKE MONEY AS A FREELANCE WRITER

7 Simple Steps to Start Your Freelance Writing Business and Earn Your First $1,000

Gina Horkey and Sally Miller

FREE BONUS

As a thank you for reading our book, we've created a list of **200+ freelance writing niches (and sub-niches)** for you to choose from.

This list is based on over 5 years of personal experience (and after working with hundreds of freelance writers). It's sure to spark some new ideas and provide you with the inspiration you need to get started writing for the web today!

Download your bonus here: tinyurl.com/fwbookbonus

Copyright © 2018 Sally Miller and Gina Horkey

All rights reserved. No part of this publication may be reproduced, distributed, or transmitted in any form or by any means, including photocopying, recording, or other electronic or mechanical methods, without the prior written permission of the publisher, except in the case of brief quotations embodied in reviews and certain other non-commercial uses permitted by copyright law.

The information provided within this book is for general informational purposes only. While the authors try to keep the information up-to-date and correct, there are no representations or warranties, express or implied, about the completeness, accuracy, reliability, suitability or availability with respect to the information, products, services, or related graphics contained in this book for any purpose. Any use of this information is at your own risk.

Any advice that is provided in this book is based on the experience of the authors and does not reflect the opinion of Amazon. All opinions expressed in this book are solely the opinion of the authors.

Disclaimer

Some of the links in this book may be affiliate links. If you click them and decide to buy something, we may be paid a commission. This won't cost you any extra. We only include links to products or services that we either use or would happily use ourselves.

CONTENTS

Free Bonus 2
CHAPTER 1 7
    Freelance Writing Challenges 8
    How to Start Your Freelance Writing Business 8
    The Seven Steps to Start Your Freelance Business 9
CHAPTER 2 11
    Fear Busting Method #1: Develop a Writing Habit 12
    Fear Busting Method #2: One Step at a Time 13
    Fear Busting Method #3: Join a Community 13
    Fear Busting Method #4: Read Your Previous Work 14
    Fear Busting Method #5: Keep Learning 14
    Fear Busting Method #6: The Bad First Draft 15
    Fear Busting Method #7: Accept Failure 15
    Three Easy to Overcome Fears 16
    Three Fears All Writers Struggle With 16
    Action Steps 17
CHAPTER 3 18
    Why Niching Down is a Good Thing 18
    How to Pick Your Niche(s) 19
    What If I Have Nothing to Write About? 20
    Another Way to Niche Down 21
    Some More Examples of Writing Niches 22
    Action Steps 23
CHAPTER 4 24
    Method #1: Search for Existing Writing Samples 25
    Method #2: Write Your Samples from Scratch 25
    Method #3: Start Your Own Blog and Website 26

- Method #4: Guest Post on Someone Else's Website 27
- Method #5: Get Started Writing for Free 28
- Method #6: Make a Paying Gig Your First Sample 28
- Action Steps 29

CHAPTER 5 30
- Do You Have to Have Your Own Website? 30
- Portfolio Method #1: A One-Pager 31
- Portfolio Method #2: A Hire Me Page 32
- Portfolio Method #3: Pinterest 33
- Portfolio Method #4: Contently 34
- Action Steps 35

CHAPTER 6 36
- Am I *Really* Ready? 36
- Where Do I Find Potential Jobs to Apply for? 37
- Job Source #1: Networking 37
- Job Source #2: Job Boards 38
- Job Source #3: Cold Pitching 39
- Job Source #4: Social Media 40
- Action Steps 41

CHAPTER 7 43
- My First Pitch Template 44
- My Second Pitch Template: An Okay Rendition 44
- My Current Pitch 45
- A Few Thoughts on the Progression 46
- Pitching Tip #1: Accurately Portray Your Experience 46
- Pitching Tip #2: Be Somewhat Personal 47
- Pitching Tip #3: Personalize Your Pitch 47
- Pitching Tip #4: Follow Directions Implicitly 48
- Efficiency Tip #1: Keep a Sample Pitch in Your Email Draft Folder 48
- Efficiency Tip #2: 10 by 10 49
- Efficiency Tip #3: The Early Bird Gets the Worm 49
- Efficiency Tip #4: Create a System for Following Up 50
- Action Steps 51

CHAPTER 8 52
- Freelance Writing Rates 52
- Per Word, Per Hour, or Per Article? 53
- Negotiating 54

Negotiation Tip #1: Be Confident 54
Negotiation Tip #2: Know Your Worth 55
Negotiation Tip #3: It's Easier to Ask for More Money Up Front Than It Is to Ask for a Raise 55
    Contracts 56
    Non-Disclosure Agreements (NDA) 56
    Who Typically Asks for NDAs? 57
    Writers' Agreements (Contracts) 57
    Do You Really Need a Contract? 58
    Contracts Trump All 58
    Action Steps 59

CHAPTER 9 61
    A Word About Fear 61
    The Writing Process 62
    My Self-Editing Process 63
    Article Structure 63
    More About Writing Conventions 64
    Headlines that Wow 65
    Headline Template #1: Curiosity 66
    Headline Template #2: Benefit or Solution to an Urgent Problem 66
    Headline Template #3: Fear 66
    Headline Template #4: Controversy 67
    Headline Template #5: Lists and Numbers 67
    Delivering Your Assignment and Getting Paid 67
    Action Steps 68

CHAPTER 10 69
    What Business Structure Do You Need? 70
    Accounting for Your Business 71
    Paying Taxes 72
    Beyond Your First Client 73
    Your Turn 74

About Sally Miller 75
About Gina Horkey 76

CHAPTER 1

The Magic of Beginnings

Sally Miller

*And suddenly you know: it's time to start
something new and trust the magic of beginnings.
- Meister Eckhart*

When you begin an adventure, you're filled with hope. The future holds promise. Your excitement gives you momentum. You're ready to take on the world. This is the magic of a new beginning.

You picked up this book because you're searching for a beginning. You dream about earning a living as a writer.

Perhaps you need a flexible career that allows you to stay home with your kids. Or you want to earn money as you travel the world. Maybe you long to quit your nine to five job.

Whatever your reasons, you want to make money doing something you love—writing.

Everyone's journey is different. It's possible you've always enjoyed writing, yet never thought you could make money from your passion. Or perhaps you're like me. You discovered a love for writing by accident.

I enjoyed writing as a kid, but the school system in the U.K. forces students to specialize early. I picked the sciences. And soon my time was taken up with experiments, equations, and methods. There was no space left for writing.

When I graduated, I followed a career in Information Technology, my childhood love for writing forgotten.

Then something happened. I was home with a new baby, searching for ways to occupy my mind while earning some money. I attended an online conference for writers and came away inspired.

Four months later, I'd written and published my first book. Then I wrote another one. I enjoyed writing so much, I started to freelance. I found clients who were willing to pay me to write.

At last, I'd discovered a way to pay the bills while doing something I loved.

FREELANCE WRITING CHALLENGES

My journey wasn't simple. I encountered many challenges along the way. Some of these I overcame and some I learned to live with.

As you contemplate starting a career as a freelance writer, you probably share some of my concerns.

You don't know how to get started or how much to charge.

You're afraid of failing. You don't want to tell friends and family that you followed your dreams for nothing.

You're scared of rejection. You ask yourself, what if you can't find clients? What if your clients hate your work?

I've faced all these fears and more. But I've learned that if you want something enough, you can get past your doubts.

In the next chapter, I discuss the most common concerns. I share stories from other freelance writers who've done exactly what you hope to do. All of them faced their fears and started freelance writing careers.

HOW TO START YOUR FREELANCE WRITING BUSINESS

I learned everything I needed to know from my co-author, Gina Horkey.

I first met Gina when I took her Freelance Writing Course. I was impressed by how quickly she'd found success in her career. Just six months after starting, Gina was earning over $4,000 per month.

I decided that I would learn from Gina and try freelance writing for myself. I took her course and followed the process she taught. It's the same system we describe in this book.

In my third month, I earned $1,100 while staying home with two young children. I had little free time for writing. Between diapers and naps, I could barely spare an hour per day for my new business.

I can't predict how long it will take you to earn your first $1,000. It depends on how much time you commit to the process. But what I *do* know is this—if I can do it, so can you.

This book is not for experienced writers who are further along in their career. It's also not for people who aren't prepared to follow the steps and do the work.

However, if you're one hundred percent committed to starting a freelance writing business, then this book *is* for you.

THE SEVEN STEPS TO START YOUR FREELANCE BUSINESS

So, how does this book work?

We've organized it into a series of sequential steps. We've done this so that you know exactly what to do and when to do it.

Gina wrote the middle chapters and I wrote the opening and closing chapters. You'll notice a change of writing style from one chapter to the next. We're two different people with very different styles. We think that's a good thing, since you get to benefit from both of our experiences!

The steps to start your freelance writing business are:

> Step 1: Pick your writing niche(s)
> Step 2: Gather writing samples
> Step 3: Create a portfolio
> Step 4: Source jobs
> Step 5: Start pitching
> Step 6: Land your first client
> Step 7: Earn your first $1,000

In each chapter, we explain what to do and how to do it. We include concrete action items for you to follow. If you consistently take action, then you will see results. It may take 30 days or it may take 90 days. But you will earn $1,000 as a freelance writer.

There is demand for your writing skills. According to the U.S. Bureau of Labor Statistics, in 2015 the median wage for freelance writers was $60,250. The top 10 percent earned over $114,530. Given that one in four writers work part-time, this is a healthy living for someone doing work that they love.

Now it's your turn. Read the next chapter and face your fears. Then take the first step to start your freelance writing business.

Remember, you're not alone. We and hundreds of other writers have already taken these steps and are living our dream. Don't wait until tomorrow. Start today.

CHAPTER 2

Overcoming Your Fear

Sally Miller

Stephen King once said, "The scariest moment is always just before you start. After that, things can only get better."

We all struggle with self-doubt. When I asked a freelance writing group, "What was your biggest fear starting out?" I received many heartfelt responses.

Here are some of the replies:

> *What if I'm not good enough at this to make any money? What if I can't find anything to write about that people want to read?*
> *Rejection is the biggest fear, I believe. Both from editors/clients and from announcing to society that you're a writer. There's always that idea in the back of your head that you're a fraud and someone's going to point it out.*
> *It's been my dream for so long, but what if I'm not actually a skilled writer? And then my kids starve.*
> *I'm afraid I'll only find work that pays pennies.*
> *I'm afraid my greatest passion will become my greatest failure.*
> *If I had to talk specifically about fear, I'd say failure. Maybe even a little perfectionism. What if I don't meet a client's expectations? What if I get stuck writing about something I hate?*
> *I'm just starting, and I think for me it's the fear of the unknown.*

I have shared these examples to show you that your fears are normal.

In fact, the anxiety never goes away. As your career develops, you encounter new challenges. Your old fears disappear, only to be replaced by new ones.

The secret is learning how to write in spite of your doubts.

In this chapter, I explore the most common fears faced by new freelancers. I also share strategies to overcome these fears so that you can forge a successful writing career.

Let's start by looking at seven ways to handle your fears.

FEAR BUSTING METHOD #1: DEVELOP A WRITING HABIT

I hear this advice all the time. Bloggers, podcasters, and experts all tell us to develop a daily writing habit.

It works because a habit makes a task automatic. Writing becomes something you do (almost) without thinking.

Science backs this up. A study in the British Journal of Health Psychology found that 91 percent of people who planned their intention to exercise ended up doing so. This compared to just 38 percent of people in the control group.

The message is simple. Having an intention to do something increases the likelihood of following through.

So, what does a writing habit look like? It's different for each person. For example, my writing habit has two parts.

The first part is the act of writing. I aim to write for one hour each day. I put our baby down for his morning nap and then start. I don't decide whether to write or not. I just do it.

I find it helps to determine what to write about in advance. It may be a work assignment for a client or a chapter of my next book. It doesn't matter, as long as I sit down to write at the same time each day.

The second part of my habit is to look for new work. You want to consistently seek new writing gigs. A good way to do this is to make pitching part of your regular writing habit.

I send one pitch per day. You may want to send more, especially when starting out. In chapter seven, Gina teaches you how to craft an effective pitch.

FEAR BUSTING METHOD #2: ONE STEP AT A TIME

In his bestselling book, *The One Thing*, Gary Keller explains how successful people focus on the one thing that needs to be done today.

The book you're reading right now supports this approach. We've organized it into sequential steps that will take you from novice to freelance writer.

Let's say you're on step two, gathering writing samples. You want to pour all of your energy into completing this activity. Avoid looking ahead to the next steps until you're done.

By focusing your energy on what needs to be done today, you block out everything else. You don't succumb to feeling overwhelmed. You keep moving forward, one step at a time.

FEAR BUSTING METHOD #3: JOIN A COMMUNITY

It's comforting to know you're not alone.

A writing community provides reassurance that your fears are normal. Your spouse, best friend, or parents can't understand the challenges you face. Other writers do.

Communities also provide accountability. They're a place to announce your goals and report progress. Accountability keeps you motivated even when you're struggling.

It's easy to find online writing communities by searching on Google or Facebook. For example, Gina runs a group for members of her Freelance Writing Course. I post in her group when I'm struggling or need an answer to a writing-related question.

Another option is to join a freelance writing group via websites such as Meetup.com, or look for groups by visiting your local libraries and asking around. If you can't find one, you can even start your own. Not only will you meet other local writers who can help you on your journey, it also gives you a reason to get out of your house. This can be even more valuable for a freelancer who works from home.

FEAR BUSTING METHOD #4: READ YOUR PREVIOUS WORK

This method is simple, yet effective. It's all about giving yourself a small ego boost!

When I doubt whether I can tackle a task, I look back and read what I've already written.

If you've never done this, try it now. Read something you've written. A blog post, a book chapter, even a report for your job. Any form of writing will do.

As you read the piece, remember this is your work. You can write. And you can succeed on your next assignment.

FEAR BUSTING METHOD #5: KEEP LEARNING

It's natural to seek new knowledge. That is what you're doing by reading this book. You're learning how to start your freelance writing career.

I believe the best way to learn is through practice. I recommend writing every day (see Fear Busting Method #1).

However, practice is not your only option. Many of the best sources of learning are free. You can follow blogs, read books, listen to podcasts, ask questions in communities, meet with other writers, and take courses.

I follow writers who are further along in their career than me. I like to learn from their experiences.

One word of caution, though. If you aren't applying what you're learning, it's time to stop reading and start taking action. Don't let learning get in the way of progress.

FEAR BUSTING METHOD #6: THE BAD FIRST DRAFT

Sometimes the hardest part of being a writer is getting the words out of your head and onto the page. Many new writers find themselves staring at a blank screen, struggling to get started. They write and rewrite the first sentence.

With this fear busting strategy, you let go of your perfectionism. You stop searching for the right words. You write down your thoughts as quickly as possible, without editing as you go.

Your first draft won't be great. That's okay. You're the only person who will see it, and you can refine your work later.

Once you have a page full of words, you'll feel a lot better. You'll also finish assignments faster than before.

FEAR BUSTING METHOD #7: ACCEPT FAILURE

This last strategy applies to everything you do, not just freelance writing.

You need to accept failure.

Your freelance career is a business. And in business, things go wrong. Your work will be criticized. Your proposals will be rejected.

But remember this: Rejection happens to everyone.

J. K. Rowling's agent sent the manuscript for *Harry Potter and the Philosopher's Stone* to 12 different publishers before it was accepted. If Rowling had given up, the world would not have benefited from one of the most successful book franchises in history.

When I asked about fear in a writing community, one person said this:

> *At some point, you just have to do it. But do it to the highest standards and the best of your ability. When I absolutely do my best, a rejection doesn't bother me as much. I know I tried to the best of my ability.*

This is excellent advice. If you can accept failure, nothing can stop you from succeeding.

THREE EASY TO OVERCOME FEARS

Now that you have the tools to deal with your fears, let's look at the most common roadblocks. The first fears are the easiest to overcome. They are:
1. I don't have enough time to write.
2. Writing doesn't pay enough money.
3. I don't know how to get started.

If you think you don't have enough time, think again. I started with one hour per day. You can squeeze this into your lunch break or get up early before the rest of your household is awake.

As you build a client base, you can buy more time. Pay someone to do your household chores, or quit your day job. One of the biggest benefits of freelancing is that you choose when and for how long you work.

The second fear is that you won't earn enough money. Yes, some content mills pay just $10 for one blog post. However, these aren't the only writing opportunities.

In my third month as a freelance writer, I earned $1,100. I was a stay-at-home mom and spent a few hours each week on my business. When Gina started out, her earnings were even higher.

You can do this, too. In this book, we teach you how to steer clear of the content mills and earn a real living writing. We give you the exact steps to earn your first $1,000.

THREE FEARS ALL WRITERS STRUGGLE WITH

This second group of fears is less easy to dismiss. Unlike the first group, these are real emotions that all writers struggle with. They are:
1. I'm not good enough.
2. I'm scared of failing.
3. I'm afraid of rejection.

You'll almost certainly encounter all of these fears as a freelancer. Know that you're not alone. I constantly struggle with negative thoughts, but I don't let it stop me. You shouldn't either. You *can* become a freelance writer.

I've already shared the importance of writing despite your fears. The strategies in this chapter will help you do this. You may not need to use all of them.

Instead, take each one for a test drive. Figure out what works best for you. And whatever you do, don't let fear become your master.

ACTION STEPS

1. Review the fear busting methods.
2. Pick two or three you think will work for you.

When you're ready, read the next chapter and learn the first step to starting your freelance writing business.

CHAPTER 3

Step One: Find Your Niche

Sally Miller

Before you embark on your freelance writing journey, there's one question you need to answer.

What are you going to write about?

If the idea of picking a niche is scary, don't worry. This isn't about limiting yourself.

You don't have to stick with the first area you chose. I changed my niche just three months after starting my freelance writing career. I'm still experimenting with different types of writing and expect that I'll always do so.

In fact, you don't have to choose a niche at all. Many successful freelancers write about a range of topics. But there are some good reasons to select a niche or two.

WHY NICHING DOWN IS A GOOD THING

As you explore the world of freelancing, you'll discover many opportunities. This is good. It means more ways for you to earn a living as a writer.

However, the options can be overwhelming. One way to overcome this is to narrow your focus. Pick a few subjects you're comfortable writing about and search for jobs in just those areas.

This approach helps you stand out. When you apply for a job, you can use your background to strengthen your pitch.

For example, my first niche was Airbnb vacation rentals. I'd written an Amazon best-selling book on how to make money on Airbnb. When targeting businesses in the Airbnb space, I used my book as evidence of my expertise.

Another advantage is that you develop your knowledge in your subject area. You gather resources that you can constantly draw upon and form relationships with relevant sources.

As your skill grows, you write faster. And this brings me to the best argument for niching down.

When you finish assignments in less time, you make more money for every hour you work. You can also position yourself as an expert and charge higher rates. Faster writing, plus higher rates, leads to a higher income. And what's not to like about that?

HOW TO PICK YOUR NICHE(S)

You've decided to focus on a few areas. Next, you need to pick your niche(s). For most writers, the process looks something like this:

1. You select one or two subject areas based on your hobbies, interests, work experience, areas of study, or unique experiences. Don't worry if you're stuck on this step. I have more on this below.

2. You start looking for jobs in these areas. We cover exactly how to do this in chapters four and five.

3. As you land your first few jobs, you notice which ones you enjoy and which pay the most.

4. You start to focus on the higher paying topics that also interest you.

To help you get started, we have put together a list of 200+ profitable niches (and sub niches). You can download the complete list at: tinyurl.com/fwbookbonus.

One word of warning—don't get too attached to one niche. Be open to writing about other subjects as new opportunities arise. More often than not, your writing niche will find you. You land an assignment in an area. You use that job to get more work. Before you know it, you're an expert on that topic.

WHAT IF I HAVE NOTHING TO WRITE ABOUT?

If you're thinking you have no relevant expertise, this is your fear talking. We all have unique experiences or interests we can draw upon.

In the previous chapter, I discussed the fear of not being good enough. This is normal. All writers suffer from self-doubt. Recognize your fear for what it is and move on.

Remember, one small step at a time. All you need to do right now is to pick a writing niche or two. To help you take action, below is a process you can use to brainstorm topics.

Start by asking yourself these five questions:

Question 1: *What are your hobbies (past and present)? Include everything you enjoyed doing as a child even if you no longer pursue that hobby.*

Question 2: *What subjects interest you? Pick topics that you wouldn't mind learning more about. Think about the nonfiction books you read for pleasure or the documentaries you enjoy watching.*

Question 3: *What jobs have you had in the past? List everything, even the summer job you had as a teenager.*

Question 4: *What subjects have you studied beyond high school level?*

Question 5: *What unique experiences do you have? Examples include starting a business, joining the military, dealing with trauma, participating in a sport.*

If you complete the above exercise, you'll uncover at least ten subject areas. Guaranteed!

Not all of these will be suitable writing topics. The best way to find a good niche is by giving it a try. Pick two or three subjects that most excite you. And don't worry about getting it right the first time.

Here're some ideas I came up with when I did this exercise:

Question 1: Sailing, skiing, reading, traveling, writing.

Question 2: Business, online marketing, history, productivity, earning money on the side.

Question 3: Retail, pharmaceuticals, finance, technology.

Question 4: Computer science, business.

Question 5: Started a business, wrote two books, made money on Airbnb.

There's some overlap in my list. But if you take the distinct topics, I have over ten viable writing niches.

ANOTHER WAY TO NICHE DOWN

Picking subjects to write about isn't the only way to niche down. You can also specialize in different *types* of writing.

Many people new to freelancing are surprised by how many opportunities exist. A good place to start is writing blog posts or magazine articles. This is the type of writing we focus on in this book. However, there are other options.

As you develop new skills, you can specialize in other forms of writing. Many of these pay four figures or more per assignment. Here's a partial list of writing types.

> Web Content and Blogs
> Sales Copy for Websites
> Newspaper and Magazine Articles
> Catalog or Product Descriptions
> Advertising Copy for Brochures
> Grants for Non-profits and Other Organizations
> Ebooks
> Business Plans
> Press Releases
> Technical Manuals
> White Papers
> Case Studies
> Email Marketing Campaigns
> Résumés
> Annual Reports
> Trade Magazine Articles
> Speeches
> Video Transcripts

This is a long list and some of these areas require specific training or experience. However, it's worth looking for new openings. You never know when a higher paying and interesting opportunity might come your way.

I started out writing blog posts, but I gradually shifted into other areas. One of my favorites is creating case studies for technology companies. I landed my first case study by pitching the idea to an existing client. From there I was able to attract more work in this area.

SOME MORE EXAMPLES OF WRITING NICHES

Both Gina and I focus on subjects that are an extension of our prior careers. For Gina, this is finance and for me it's technology.

I wanted to know how other people picked their niche and so I asked people in Gina's writing group to share how they decided to specialize. This is what one new freelancer said:

> *I have three niches that I'm focusing on to begin with. As I grow in my skills and clients, I'll narrow or widen the field as necessary.*
>
> *1. Personal Finance - This is an area that I need a lot of help in. So, I'm considering this a learn-as-you-go/bootstrap experience. As I'm deciphering what's out there, I'll share my experiences, both positive and negative. This is also my passion niche, something I can get excited about when I'm finding other work tedious.*
>
> *2. Résumé Editing - This was actually picked for me. I'm good at it, and after enough people said, "You should really charge for this," I decided to listen!*
>
> *3. Software Procedures - This is an extension of my nine to five job. I write documentation for software, so I'm already familiar with the language, formats, necessary software, and more. I'm hoping to expand this to automated demos, as well. A lot of burgeoning software companies need a freelancer who can translate from tech to norm, and I'm fairly skilled at that!*

I like this example because it includes three topics, all selected for different reasons. When starting out, it's a good idea to try several things before you find what sticks.

It also helps to remember that your niche may pick you. Another freelancer told me this:

> *I started out intent on focusing on medical writing because it's the area I have the most experience in.*
> *What did I end up writing about?*

> Well, I work for several Virtual Assistant clients. One of whom runs a website geared toward helping divorced men navigate the pitfalls of ending a marriage. I serve as the chief editor for that site.
> Then, I ghostwrite tech-related articles for another client. And I play the role of ghosty again for a third, writing about freelance writing.

ACTION STEPS

1. Identify ten or more potential writing niches by answering the five questions in this chapter.

2. Narrow down your list to two or three areas that you want to focus on.

If you're feeling stuck, check out our list of 200+ freelance writing niches (and sub-niches) at: tinyurl.com/fwbookbonus. This list is based on Gina's personal experience (and after working with hundreds of freelance writers). It's sure to spark some new ideas and provide you with the inspiration you need to get started writing for the web today!

Once you have your niche(s), move on to the next chapter. In step two, you'll gather writing samples. Don't worry if you're new to freelancing. Gina has some suggestions to help you get started even if you have no prior experience.

CHAPTER 4

Step Two: Gather Samples

Gina Horkey

Securing quality writing samples is instrumental when launching and growing a new freelance writing business.

Put yourself in your prospect's shoes for a moment. If you're sitting down to review applications for a writing gig, you would probably focus on a person's writing samples above anything else. It doesn't matter how impressive their résumé is or how many references they list. What matters is that they can deliver on what they say they can do—write well and on topics you're looking to hire them to write about.

But here's the thing, if you're a brand new freelance writer, you probably don't have any samples. It's a catch-22, right? You can't get a writing gig without having samples, and how can you get samples without experience?

Here are six ways others have built up their portfolio (myself included) that can work for you, too. They're ranked in order of easiest to hardest, which means there is no reason you can't start gathering your own samples today.

METHOD #1: SEARCH FOR EXISTING WRITING SAMPLES

Odds are if you enjoy writing, you already have numerous writing samples at your disposal.

Maybe you've written fiction in the past (published or not), maybe you've won a writing contest or two or maybe you're the go-to writer in your current or past company. I bet you have something sitting around that you could re-purpose into one of your first writing samples.

If the above didn't trigger anything right off the bat, consider this list of additional places you can find samples:

> Current or past volunteer opportunities (think newsletters, meeting summaries, etc.)
> Past high school or college papers (the closer to your niche, the better)
> Your (or your kid's) current or former schools (fundraising campaigns, newspaper stories, etc.)
> Your local church or another similar organization (newsletters, member listings, etc.)
> A friend or family member's website or business's marketing materials (blog posts, white papers, press releases or website copy)
> A personal blog or website (see above)

Obviously, this isn't an all-inclusive list. But hopefully it's enough to get your wheels turning, to fire up your imagination, and figure out if there's anything you've already written that can be used as one of your first writing samples. You can always change it out for something newer or more relevant in the future.

METHOD #2: WRITE YOUR SAMPLES FROM SCRATCH

One of the most overlooked sources of writing samples is creating them from scratch.

If you weren't able to find any (or any relevant) writing samples that you already have on hand, creating some from scratch should be your next step. It's an easy and cost effective way of securing your first few samples.

Although it'd be great to have these writing samples on a website or blog, you don't have to in order to get them in front of the right people. You can literally draft a sample blog post or article in Google Docs or Microsoft Word.

And if you want to get all fancy, you can download each sample as a PDF file. With Google Drive, you can also get a sharing link and have them appear "web-based," even if they don't live on a blog or website.

A Google doc, Word doc or PDF can still be a legit sample. Don't let anyone tell you otherwise. Remember, the goal is to showcase your sweet writing skills and provide a potential client with proof that you can write, and write well.

That's it. No need to overcomplicate things.

METHOD #3: START YOUR OWN BLOG AND WEBSITE

Starting your own blog and website is the next easiest way to build writing samples for your portfolio.

You don't need anyone's permission. You can write about what you want, when you want.

When you're ready, starting your own blog and website can be an extension of what we talked about above. You can add existing samples to your site, post your newly created samples as blog posts, and more.

Even better, you have full control.

However, keep in mind that even though you're not getting paid for your writing, you still want to put a lot of effort into it. If you're going to advertise it as an example of your writing skills, then it needs to be excellent.

Starting my own website and blog is exactly what I did to gather my initial writing samples. I had blogged socially since 2010 on free sites like Blogger. But when I started my own freelance writing business, I knew that I needed to start over and do it right.

I bought my own URL (HorkeyHandBook.com) and purchased a year's worth of hosting for less than a hundred bucks. Even though I'm a bit tech challenged, I was able to figure it out pretty quickly.

Not sure what to blog about? Don't worry! When I started out, I had no idea what my website was going to be about. In fact, I just wrote business type articles that I thought would serve as good samples. This worked fine for me.

My suggestion to you would be to write about the things you want to get paid to write about. Looking to get paid to write about real estate? Make sure you have a couple of samples on your site that have to do with that subject matter.

You need samples that fit what you're pitching for and publishing them to your own website is one of the easiest ways to do that.

METHOD #4: GUEST POST ON SOMEONE ELSE'S WEBSITE

Guest posting on someone else's website is a bit more impressive to a potential client than writing posts on your own blog.

Why? Someone else thought your writing was good enough to feature it on their site, which can go a long way.

The nice thing about getting a guest post published is that you don't have to have your own website to showcase online writing samples. Ultimately, you will want to create your own website, but guest posting is another way to get started without the additional cost and time it takes to launch one.

Great, but how does one go about finding guest posting opportunities? Here are a few ideas of places to look:

1. Tap into Your Network

Do you know anyone who has a blog in your sphere of influence? Does what they write about correspond with what you want to get paid to write about? If so, send them a friendly email or better yet, make a phone call and ask.

2. Turn to Google

It's as simple as opening a new browser and typing in "[Your Niche] + Write for Us." This search should bring up a bunch of websites in your niche that have open submissions for contributions. And, better yet, some of the opportunities might be paid opportunities, too.

3. Track Down Leads Through Social Media or Online Forums

Odds are if you're looking to break into freelance writing, you've started following some online business groups on Facebook, Reddit threads or are able to search applicable hashtags on Twitter. Use social media to your advantage to find blogs and websites in your niche and network your butt off to find a guest posting opportunity or five. (**Hint**: this also works for finding paid work.)

METHOD #5: GET STARTED WRITING FOR FREE

In addition to securing samples on my own website and networking with other bloggers to get my posts featured on their blogs, I sought out unpaid writing opportunities in the beginning of my freelance writing career.

Why? I wanted (and needed) the experience and I figured it'd be more impressive if I was a "regular contributor" somewhere, rather than just a one hit wonder.

I sourced out a couple of unpaid blogging gigs from job boards, the most prestigious of these being The Huffington Post. The Huffington Post (or HuffPo to those "in the know") makes for a great sample as their name is instantly recognizable. It can provide some additional exposure and you may get click-throughs to your own website.

The biggest thing HuffPo did for me was it gave me a solid sample for my portfolio that was impressive to prospects. I feel this one source legitimized me as a writer—in my own head, if nothing else.

After you've built up your client base, you could decide to continue on writing for free or, if you no longer have the time, you could quit. I've since dropped all of my free work, as I barely have the time to keep up with my paying clients' workload and my own personal projects (like this book).

METHOD #6: MAKE A PAYING GIG YOUR FIRST SAMPLE

Yep, you read that right. It's possible to get your first paying gig and your first freelance writing sample at the same time.

Easy? Maybe not. But possible? 100 percent.

Most aspiring freelance writers think they have to wait until they have all of their ducks in a row before they start pitching for paid work. I call B-S! Why not do both at the same time?

There's absolutely no reason why you can't be pitching for paying gigs while you're still gathering samples for your portfolio. While I opened with the fact that those reviewing your application will want to see samples, it's not impossible to pitch for and receive your first sample as a paid writing opportunity. (Plus, technically, your email pitch or online application/cover letter is an example of your writing capabilities...)

We'll get into where to source writing gigs in chapter six, but just know that it's been done before.

Potential writing samples are everywhere. You might already have them on hand. If you don't, create a few quick (but excellent) writing samples in Google Docs or Microsoft Word. If you're in it for the long haul, consider setting up your own website and blog.

When you're ready, start guest posting on other people's sites or acquiring your first one or two writing clients by writing for free. Lastly, it's not impossible to land your first sample as your first paid writing project. In fact, that'd be ideal.

ACTION STEPS

1. Do a little recon to see if you currently have any writing samples at your disposal from the sources listed above.

2. At a minimum, write two to three samples in Google Docs or Microsoft Word. Consider downloading them as a PDF to jazz them up as you share them with prospects.

3. Consider starting your own website and blog to both house your writing samples and practice honing your craft by publishing regular posts.

4. Source three to five websites in your niche that you can pitch a guest post idea to.

5. Stay open to writing for free (at least in the beginning) to gather samples and a testimonial.

6. Don't wait to pitch for paying work until you have sufficient samples. Dive in and get your feet wet by doing both at the same time.

So far, you've selected your niches and gathered writing samples. The next step is to create your online portfolio. And the great news is that there's more than one way to go about it. In fact, there are several. In the next chapter, I share four ways to create your portfolio.

CHAPTER 5

Step Three: Create A Portfolio

Gina Horkey

A potential client wants to see samples of your work. This is where your portfolio comes in.

You get to choose how you display your portfolio. You can use as much or as little creativity as you'd like so that you stand out from the pack. Let your freak flag fly (if you have one) and go with the option that best fits your creative expression and your budget.

Or maybe you'll try more than one of them. Do you, girlfriend (or boyfriend)!

DO YOU HAVE TO HAVE YOUR OWN WEBSITE?

In step two, on gathering samples, we talked about starting your own website and blog as one way to secure samples and showcase them. And while I believe it's important to have an Internet home, someplace you can direct potential clients to see samples of your work, you don't have to have your own website.

Would I recommend that you do (at least eventually)?

Yep.

Websites are today's equivalent of a business card. Of course, whether or not you have one depends more on what your overall or long-term goals are when it comes to online business. Do you just want to showcase a writing portfolio or are you interested in building a website you can monetize down the road?

Having said that, you don't absolutely have to have a website.

Now that we have that out of the way, let's look at four ways that you can display your online writing portfolio and the costs associated with each. Three out of the four are free—score!

PORTFOLIO METHOD #1: A ONE-PAGER

One of the simplest ways to house your online portfolio is by creating a one (or two) pager.

Basically, it's a Google or Word doc that you can download as a PDF and which has its own unique url that you can easily share (ideally via a hyperlink) with others.

What should you include?

You can include whatever you want.

I have some blogging statistics (which are great if you're trying convince a company or client to add a blog to a website that doesn't have one), my headshot and bio, some general rate information, the services I offer, my main writing niches, and a call to action (CTA) at the end to urge them to get in touch.

Benefits of a one-pager:

> It's FREE.
> It can be updated easily and at any time.
> Anyone can print it off for a physical copy.
> You can get super creative with it if you want.

Drawbacks of a one-pager:

> Each time you change the Google or Word doc, you'll need to download it as a new PDF. This changes the link associated with the doc.
> You need to keep it updated for it to remain relevant. For example, don't forget to update your rates as you increase them!

Side Note: Google Drive/Docs is amazing and free to use. Better yet, you can access your documents from any computer, as long as you log in and have Internet access. It's one of my favorite online tools. It includes Google versions of Microsoft Word, Excel, PowerPoint, and more. Drive is usually compatible with the Microsoft and Mac versions of these programs, and you can easily share with others via email or by getting a unique URL for the piece of content.

PORTFOLIO METHOD #2: A HIRE ME PAGE

If you're going to go for your own website, you need to secure your own URL (web address) and have it be self-hosted. That means a free Blogger or WordPress account won't cut it. It doesn't always look professional and you're better off doing it right from the start.

I set up my own website and Hire Me page right away. I made the mistake of buying my domain name and hosting services separately. Although there weren't any lasting effects, it made it more confusing than it had to be. From what I've gleaned over the last several years, there aren't many differences between large web hosting providers.

The total cost was under $100 for the first year (and every year thereafter). This is more than worth it since we make *all* of our household income online. I update my Hire Me page periodically (more frequently when I was building my client base or breaking into new niches) to keep it fresh and relevant.

Just like how a blog's About page isn't about the blog owner (it's about the reader and confirming they're in the right place), your Hire Me page is more about your potential client than it is about you. Your goal is to make them feel welcomed, assured they're in the right spot, and intrigued enough that they'll read through your service offerings and hopefully click on your CTA.

I start mine out with a compelling headline/question, benefits that the prospect should be interested in, highlight the various niches I write in (including samples underneath), and end with another CTA to get in touch. Just like on the one-pager, I have a photograph. Clients want to connect with a real person, not a secret possible human. They want to get to know who they're hiring and what better way to do that than show them a photo with your pearly whites?

One thing that is different on my Hire Me page (than on my one-pager) is that I advertise social proof in the "As Seen On" section. These are high-profile sites that I've been published on in the past. Social proof is powerful, which is why my website also has a Client Testimonials page.

Benefits of a Hire Me page:

> Having your own website/blog is impressive to clients, especially if they want you to work in the backend of theirs. It shows that you're already familiar with WordPress.

> A website or Hire Me page can be updated easily and at any time.

> The link will remain the same regardless of how many edits you make to the page.

> You can completely customize a WordPress site with skills (or a tech guy!)

Drawbacks of a Hire Me page:

> It's not free.
> Creating your own website has a steep learning curve for those of us who are not tech-savvy.

PORTFOLIO METHOD #3: PINTEREST

When I started my freelance writing business, my Hire Me page was my main portfolio.

But it wasn't much later that I learned that Pinterest was a viable (and aesthetically pleasing) option for also displaying an online freelance writing portfolio. I added a second portfolio via one of the hottest social media platforms of the decade.

I've received a lot of compliments on my Pinterest board and I'd recommend starting one either way. It's free and it's easy to set up. And there's the added bonus that your samples can be re-pinned and shared socially. Who doesn't chomp at the bit at the possibility of one's work going viral?

Plus, the more social shares your work has, the more desired you'll be as a writer. It's another way to prove your writing skills and market yourself.

There's not much you can do with a Pinterest board beyond pinning the links or images of your articles and re-pinning them. Of course, you'll want to make full use of your bio and each pin's description. Beyond that, there's not a lot of customization allowed on the platform.

Again, I'd recommend you start a Pinterest portfolio and play around with it. Even if it doesn't remain your main online portfolio (mine isn't), my guess is that you'll learn a thing or two about Pinterest. This will translate positively into your new freelance writing business in one way or another.

Benefits of a Pinterest portfolio:
> It's FREE.
> It can be updated easily and at any time.
> It's a visually appealing portfolio option.
> Your samples can get re-pinned and potentially go viral.

Drawbacks of a Pinterest portfolio:
> It's not customizable.
> If you're not good at creating graphics, you might need some image help.

PORTFOLIO METHOD #4: CONTENTLY

I've saved the best for last.

Contently is probably my *favorite* online portfolio option of the moment. It's free, it's beautiful, and the best part is that you might catch the eye of a Contently editor and get hired to write for their clients.

How great is that?

It doesn't happen right away, but my Contently portfolio was picked up by an editor around six months after I published it. The client I wrote for paid well. *Very well*—over $500 for a 500- to 900-word post in the personal finance niche.

It's also cool that they list how many articles and words you've written, as well as the number of social shares and views your work has seen. Remember that whole social proof thing we've been talking about? Contently has it nailed down. I love this social proof concept and think potential employers do, too.

I have a post on my blog, HorkeyHandbook.com, about getting picked up by the Contently team. Here are a couple of highlights if you don't have the time to read it through: Only add your best stuff, specify your niche in your bio section, and showcase your best niche, rather than random samples from random niches.

Benefits of a Contently portfolio:

> It's FREE.
> It can be updated easily and at any time.
> It's beautiful.
> You have the chance of catching the eye of the Contently team and being hired to write for their clients (at a super good rate!).
> The platform is intuitive.

Drawbacks of a Contently portfolio:

> You might not want to post samples from all of your niches to your portfolio.
> You need to keep it updated for it to remain relevant and get noticed by the Contently team.
> It's not customizable.
> You may have to manually add photos, descriptions, and more if the platform doesn't pick them up.

Having an online portfolio is a must.

In step three, we talked about four different ways to display yours—via a one- or two-page PDF, your own website, a Pinterest board, or a Contently portfolio. I've tried them all, but I favor my Hire Me page and Contently portfolio.

Do what you feel comfortable with. Also, what fits your budget and appeals to you the most. You can always try more than one (or all) of the suggestions listed here to see what you like best or to display different types of portfolios for different niches or clients.

Start with displaying any samples you currently have and then add new samples as you acquire them. And don't forget to get creative and have some fun with it.

ACTION STEPS

1. Decide which medium you'd like to start with for your online portfolio.
2. Add any samples you currently have.
3. Add any future samples to your portfolio option of choice.
4. Feel free to experiment with more than one to see which you like the best.

Next up, I talk about where to find writing gigs. If you want to start earning money as a writer, you need to be constantly sourcing jobs and pitching. I'll cover exactly how to do this in the next two chapters.

CHAPTER 6

Step Four: Source Jobs

Gina Horkey

So far, our steps have covered deciding on your freelance writing niche(s), gathering a few samples and establishing your online portfolio. Now it's time to put your research skills to work and source writing jobs to apply for.

In chapter seven, I focus on actually sending a pitch (or job inquiry/application), so don't get ahead of yourself. In this chapter, we're going to tackle where to look for work.

AM I *REALLY* READY?

You might be asking yourself this question right about now. In my opinion, there's no time like the present. Rip that Band-Aid off and go for it!

As we've already discussed, it's normal to feel afraid. To be unsure if you're good enough. Or to be a bit nervous about getting rejected.

I'll let you in on a little secret. It's going to happen. A lot.

You're going to get told "no," more times than you'll hear "yes." And that's okay. Because there's this whole big sea called the Internet full of potential prospect fish for you to hook.

Not to get all cheesy on you, but it's true. Opportunities for freelance writers are limitless. In fact, one of my favorite sayings right now (that I totally came up with) is:

> *"Every business needs a website and virtually every website is in need of a decent writer."*

Even if you don't feel ready, you are. You have to be. Because if not now, then when?

One of my other favorite quotes—not by me—is:

> *"Never give up on a dream just because of the time it will take to accomplish it. The time will pass anyway."* – Earl Nightingale

WHERE DO I FIND POTENTIAL JOBS TO APPLY FOR?

Now that we've determined you're as ready as you'll ever be, the next question you should be asking is where to find jobs.

Again, I'll address all of your questions about what your pitch should look like in the next chapter, so let's just focus on where to find opportunities and start compiling a list. I'm going to give you four distinct ways to prospect for clients.

You in? Awesome, let's get started.

JOB SOURCE #1: NETWORKING

Have you ever heard, "Your network is your net worth?"

It's kind of true, right? The premise is that who you know is more valuable than the money you have sitting in the bank. You can tap into your existing network to find a new job, connect with new clients, and more. That's invaluable.

If you have successful businesspeople in your sphere, I recommend that you take them to lunch, to coffee or at a minimum ask for a quick phone chat (try to avoid email as much as possible for this exercise). See if they have a few minutes available so you can pick their brain about marketing or business advice in general.

Don't ask them for work, but instead ask for their help. Let them know who your ideal clients are (refer to the niches you selected in step one) and ask that they keep you in mind if a relevant opportunity crops up. It's not about finding an immediate job, but rather planting the seed and letting them know exactly who you're looking for in a client.

People love to help.

Don't worry if you don't know the right people. I didn't (and probably still don't). And I was still able to build a successful freelance writing business.

Even if you don't have an existing network to tap into, it doesn't mean that you can't build one. Research your local Chamber of Commerce, attend a few applicable Meetups where you can get in touch with your target market, or check out networking groups in your area.

Again, the goal isn't to land immediate business. It's to start the relationship building process. To become an authority in your niche and the go-to freelance writer around. It takes time, but it can pay off for years to come if you do it right.

JOB SOURCE #2: JOB BOARDS

A second way to source writing gigs is to work online job boards.

I'm not gonna lie, there are many freelance writing experts who hate job boards. And for good reason—they don't always offer the best rates, there are hundreds of other freelancers submitting pitches, and once in a while there's a scam listed.

The reason I like them, though, is that job boards are what I used to land 90 percent of my freelance writing gigs in the beginning. For many, including myself, it was easier to pitch clients who had an active listing. They were looking to hire a freelance writer for a specific writing project.

This is also a great way to practice your pitching skills, such as experimenting with your subject lines to see what gets the most open rates and following specific directions. This helps you to get to know what clients are looking for in a writer. You can tweak your pitch based on your response rate, you get to practice negotiating, and it's low risk.

Job boards are *not* content mills, which try to get writers to do large volumes of work for low pay. If you want to give job boards a try, here are four that I recommend. Three are free options and one is paid.

Side Note: I used the free sources for the first couple of weeks, but then moved on to the paid versions because I had limited time to grow my business. I decided to pay a little to get quality leads and search one site versus many.

The three free sites are:

ProBlogger

JournalismJobs

Craigslist (Chicago, San Francisco, and Manhattan are great cities to start with)

Contena is the paid option I recommend. It's a powerful tool built for freelance writers and content creators. The platform makes it easy for you to find and compare the best writing and editing jobs across multiple popular sites, as well as sort by company, category, quality, and even rate. You're also able to apply alerts and follow companies. This tool will do the work for you and send you an email when something meets your criteria.

One of the reasons I like Contena so much is that Kevin, Contena's co-founder, is motivated to provide a quality experience for the site's users. He used to hire hundreds of freelance writers each year and his wife is actually a professional writer. They know a thing or two about this industry and what it takes to succeed.

They've recently added coaching services to ensure your pitching game is boss and landing you clients. Your Contena coach will work with you to assemble an effective pitch, refine your portfolio, and can show you exactly what's working for their most successful members.

Bonus: If you use the coupon code "horkey10" at checkout, you'll save 10 percent off the cost of any package.

JOB SOURCE #3: COLD PITCHING

As I mentioned, most of my early success was from using job boards. But since then, I've moved on to other methods, like networking, asking clients for referrals, and cold pitching companies.

Many of my coaching clients have also had a lot of success cold pitching. You control your prospect pool (remember, every company needs a website and virtually every website needs a decent writer) and you can target companies without blogs, with inactive blogs as well as those that have a thriving and active online presence.

What is cold pitching? It's basically reaching out to companies directly, finding out if they have any current (or future) writing needs, and pitching yourself as the go-to writer when the opportunity arises. Some may think it's a bit ballsy, but I prefer to think of it as smart.

Remember those reservations other freelance writing experts had about job boards? Well, cold pitching alleviates all of them. Since there is no job listing online, odds are that you're one of the only (if not the only) person approaching a company at any given time for freelance writing work. Now, you take the risk that they're not in need of a writer, but by starting the conversation and building a relationship, you're increasing your odds of being remembered when and if they do have a need in the future.

The competition is nil, which is great. What's also great is that since you're taking charge and doing your own prospecting, you can also take charge when it comes to negotiating rates. Some clients don't have a clue on what the going rate is for a freelance writer and they're probably not looking for the cheapest price (which often correlates to the value delivered) when it comes to hiring a freelance writer.

Lastly, unlike with job boards, your leads are unlimited. You can research 50 different companies per day (or per week or per month) to pitch and not run out for years or decades to come. There are always new companies forming.

Cold pitching could be an entire book in itself, so this section is meant to give you a high-level view of what it is and how you can get started. Here are a few additional tips:

> Pitching in general is a numbers game. The more you send out, the more likely you'll be to land a client.

> Just like with networking, focus on building a relationship through cold pitching before asking for work.

> Follow-up is key (we'll talk more about this in the next chapter). You can't just send one pitch email and expect to get work. Often, it takes multiple attempts to even get the first reply.

JOB SOURCE #4: SOCIAL MEDIA

I got one of my earliest freelance writing clients via a Facebook group.

In hindsight, it wasn't the best gig of my portfolio (I ghostwrote some gluten-free blog posts). But I learned a lot through the experience. It was one of my first paying clients, it was my first ghostwriting project, and she wanted to work through UpWork (then Elance) for payment protection.

That experience forced me to set up a profile on the platform and learn how to use it. Even though I wasn't super active on Elance, I did get a great client off the platform a few months later—and they sought me out!

Regardless, social media can be a great way to source job leads. That early opportunity came about because I put myself out there. I let people know that I was a freelance writer and kept my eyes open for leads.

As opportunities popped up, I jumped on them. And that would be my main advice to you, too. If you don't tell people that you're a writer-for-hire, they won't think to hire you or refer you to someone they know who's looking for one.

It's not good enough to do it just once, either. You should regularly (and creatively) let people know that you're taking on new clients (without looking desperate).

Some freelance writers will comment on a project they're working on. Others will share valuable articles with their target market. There are a host of ways to connect with prospects socially. Figure out what platforms you want to be on (less is more) and learn how to use them to your full advantage as a new freelance writer looking for work.

I'm full of favorite sayings in this chapter, but another one of mine is #AlwaysBeMarketing.

Constantly keep your eyes and ears open for new opportunities. This is how I snagged that gig in the Facebook group. And it's what you should do, too.

If Facebook is your thing, join some applicable groups in your niche. Then peruse them regularly for opportunities (you can also use the search function) to respond to a need or just be authentically helpful. This is a great way to start building relationships so you'll be remembered.

If Facebook is not your thing, figure out the trending hashtags on Twitter or search terms in LinkedIn. There's a platform (or two) for everyone, so figure out which one suits your needs, learn the ins and outs of it, and then plug it into your schedule to do a little recon/relationship building on a daily (or at least weekly) basis.

There are multiple ways to search for freelance writing work.

I've listed four methods: networking, job boards, cold pitching, and social media. Try them all and see what you like doing best and, more importantly, what method(s) get you the best results. Remember, there's no time like the present to get started.

ACTION STEPS

1. Sit down with at least three people from your network to pick their brains about launching/marketing your new freelance writing business.

2. Start perusing job boards for writing gigs in the niches you defined earlier on in this book.

3. After you've given job boards a try, start cold pitching on a regular basis. You might not hear back from people right away, but you never know when today's effort will turn into tomorrow's profit.

4. Start prospecting via social media on a daily or weekly basis. #AlwaysBeMarketing.

Once you have a list of potential jobs, you're ready to start pitching. In the next chapter, I show you how to pitch like a pro and get results.

CHAPTER 7

Step Five: Start Pitching

Gina Horkey

Having a great pitch is what will separate you from the crowd when competing against other freelancers (in the case of job board ads) or against yourself (when cold pitching, for example).

My pitch has come a long way since I began sending it out in May of 2014. It has gone through dozens of revisions. In fact, I probably updated it weekly for a while.

Why? Because as I learned what was working, or more accurately what wasn't, I modified it accordingly. I kept track of my "batting average" and wanted to get it as close to 1,000 as possible.

I thought you'd benefit most from a timeline of sorts, so here are three different pitch examples that I actually sent out. The last being the closest to the one I'm currently using.

MY FIRST PITCH TEMPLATE

> *Good Morning,*
> *I would love to throw my hat into the ring for this freelance writing position.*
> *I'm a regular Huffington Post contributor and currently am writing copy for a major WordPress blog.*
> *I'm confident that I would be a great addition to your team. Please let me know what else I can provide you with.*
> *Gina Horkey*

MY SECOND PITCH TEMPLATE: AN OKAY RENDITION

> *Hi, Mrs. Smith,*
> *I was really excited to read your job listing for a freelance writer. I think I'm a perfect fit!*
> *A little about me personally: I'm a mom to two toddlers and live with my spouse (a SAHD) in Minnesota. Productivity, therefore, is the name of the game!*
> *I've been working in the financial services industry for the past eight years and am currently in the process of transitioning to full-time freelance writing as my main career. I can easily write about various topics, in addition to personal finance.*
> *I regularly contribute to The Huffington Post, Remedy Lending, and Kitchology. I've built and run my own website and blog, and I've been blogging since early 2010.*
> *Here are three posts from my own blog specifically about productivity. The above links showcase additional work.*
> *> http://horkeyhandbook.com/just-getting-unpleasant-tasks-done/*

> http://horkeyhandbook.com/pomodoro-technique-productivity-hack/
> http://horkeyhandbook.com/a-taste-of-working-from-the-road/

I'm currently also ghostwriting for numerous large freelance websites and have recently launched a new project with a friend, called Young Widow Living.

I'm confident that I would be a great addition to your writing team. I'm very detail oriented and mindful of time management and meeting deadlines.

<WRITING RESUME>

Please let me know if I can provide you with anything else. Check out my "Hire Me" page for client testimonials and my Professional Writing Pinterest Board for additional samples.

Gina Horkey

MY CURRENT PITCH

Hey, [NAME],

Your ad on [PLACE YOU SAW AD] immediately caught my attention. I'm a professional writer with experience in [YOUR RELEVANT EXPERIENCE] and I'd love to work with you.

[Insert some notes on company if disclosed after perusing their website and make a connection or authentically compliment them.]

More about me/my experience:
> My Hire Me page for samples/niches that I specialize in
> My Client Testimonials' page for references
> My Portfolio for additional samples

Or take a look at the three publications I've written for regularly to see some of my work:
> The Huffington Post
> Go Banking Rates
> Double Your Freelancing

> [Alternatively, you could list three specific blog post titles that match what they're looking for in a writer.]
> Additionally, I've:
> > Built and run my own website and blog.
> > Been blogging since early 2010.
> > Wrote the copy and press release for this Kickstarter campaign, which was fully funded within one week and went on to be funded five times over within a month.
> I'm confident that I would be a great addition to your writing team. I'm very detail oriented and mindful of time management and meeting deadlines.
> Hit reply to continue the conversation.
> – Gina

A FEW THOUGHTS ON THE PROGRESSION

I'm sure you can see my pitch has gotten stronger over time.

You might also notice that my first pitch was a little too short and sweet. And it didn't include *any* links, probably because I didn't have any. *No bueno!*

The second pitch was a bit too long. People have short attention spans. It wasn't converting like a previous version that I had sent, so I figured it was time for a redo.

The most current version gets a fair amount of positive attention, meaning it's converting into new clients. Although I'm sure that I'll continue to update it over time, it's a solid representation of what I've got going on at the moment.

Now that I've shared my evolution of pitches, I want to give you four tips to make your pitch as good as possible (even if you don't have a ton of experience).

PITCHING TIP #1: ACCURATELY PORTRAY YOUR EXPERIENCE

One main part of my pitch hasn't changed much over time.

I highlight that I've been blogging since 2010 and it's completely true. I just haven't been blogging for money since 2010.

I started blogging socially in March of 2010 to chronicle my experience through the P90X workout program. I had been reading other health and fitness blogs for some time, and I loved to write, so I thought, "Why not?"

The truth of the matter is that I only blogged for socialization and accountability. I wasn't trying to get paid for my writing or develop a huge following.

Even though my blogging wasn't income producing, it was huge in helping me learn some of the basics of writing for the web. And now I can say that I've been a blogger for over six years.

PITCHING TIP #2: BE SOMEWHAT PERSONAL

Yes, your pitch should be professional. It should not be totally informal or highlight what you ate for lunch. But it can help to be a little personal.

As you can see from above, for a while I included that I was a mom to two toddlers, that my husband was a stay-at-home dad, and that we lived in Minnesota. My goal in disclosing this information was to connect on some level with the person hiring. I wanted them to visualize that I was more than some random person sending them an email pitch for a job.

I don't include these exact details in my initial pitch anymore, but I'm not hiding them or my personality either. If you have something that connects with the particular writing gig you're applying for, don't hesitate to share.

Making some sort of lasting impression is better than being easily forgotten. Give yourself a chance at being remembered.

PITCHING TIP #3: PERSONALIZE YOUR PITCH

If the hiring manager includes their name in the pitch details, or it's obvious via their email address, make sure to address them accordingly.

If it's a job that you're especially interested in, it doesn't hurt to do a little research on the company and add a specific compliment or two either. Do your homework and strategically show that you did by personalizing your pitch.

The key here is that you're authentic and you know what you're talking about. Don't go to their website, read the first paragraph of their last post, and comment without knowing more about what they have going on. Look a little deeper than that.

PITCHING TIP #4: FOLLOW DIRECTIONS IMPLICITLY

If a pitch says to submit three samples and your résumé, you'd better submit three samples and your résumé. Read directions (a few times if you need to) and make sure to respond to each job listing with exactly what they want from you.

Many potential employers will weed out applicants this way. They'll ask for a specific email subject line or for you to include your fee or something else. If you're going to take the time to apply for a job, you might as well do it right.

Now that your pitch is decent, let's talk about a few habits you should adopt to be as efficient as possible in your pitching.

EFFICIENCY TIP #1: KEEP A SAMPLE PITCH IN YOUR EMAIL DRAFT FOLDER

Take what you've learned so far and draft a sample pitch email. Save this as an email draft, so you can copy and paste it in the future when applying to new freelance writing jobs.

This one step has saved me so much time. I know my pitch is ready to go at any time. When I find a job I want to apply for, all I need to do is start a new email, paste my sample pitch text into it, and then customize it to fit the specific writing position. Works like a charm.

Pro Tip: If you use Gmail, you can also set up canned responses.

EFFICIENCY TIP #2: 10 BY 10

I can't exactly take credit for this one. I read this tip on someone else's blog, but don't remember where.

The basic premise is that you send out ten pitches by ten o'clock in the morning. Feel free to modify to meet your exact needs; I did. I think the general concept, though, is spot-on.

Let's say that it takes you 50 pitches to get one new client. Realistically, if you pitched 10 new jobs, five days per week, you would get one new client each week. If you pitched only five per day, then you would only wind up with half as many clients, or on average one every other week.

Regardless of what your conversion ratio currently is, the concept speaks to being proactive and consistent with your pitching efforts. It's a numbers game. The more you pitch, the more clients you'll land.

If you're just getting started and don't have a batting average yet, pitch as much as you possibly can. Your number one goal is to get clients, and pitching is how you'll accomplish that at first.

EFFICIENCY TIP #3: THE EARLY BIRD GETS THE WORM

When it comes to answering job board ads, it's been said that the earlier you submit your pitch (compared to when it's listed), the better your odds are of getting the position. I've found this to be true with my own pitching experience.

When a client is ready to hire someone, they were usually ready yesterday. They have a need *now*. The closer you submit your pitch to when they place the listing, the better your chances are of getting hired.

This means that you should be checking your lead sources daily for new listings. It also means that you shouldn't sit on a lead and wait until your pitch is perfect. There's no such thing as a perfect pitch. The best way to increase your odds of success are to submit a good-enough pitch sooner, rather than later.

EFFICIENCY TIP #4: CREATE A SYSTEM FOR FOLLOWING UP

I have gotten a couple of clients just based on my ability to follow up with them after we've had an initial exchange. Clients are busy and they can drop the ball when it comes to email, filling a job, and more.

There's also the off-chance that they hired someone they're not completely happy with. Believe it or not, there are a fair amount of unresponsive and irresponsible freelance writers out there. Just being proactive about communication can go a long way.

When I apply to a new writing job and someone responds to me personally (not through a form letter), I usually thank them for their response and file the email in my "Awaiting Reply" folder. If I haven't heard anything for a while, or based on the date they said I would, I follow up with a short and sweet email saying that I'm circling back to see if they've filled *xyz* writing position.

Then I try to go through my "Awaiting Reply" email folder at least one or two times a week to follow up. There are many times that I don't get a response, but I like to know definitively either way. There have been a few times that my polite persistence has paid off and they've decided to award me the job.

Pro Tip: My friend Joe subscribes to the rule of following up 10 times before declaring the lead dead.

Having a stellar pitch is key.

Once you do, there are ways you can make the pitching process more turn-key. By creating your own system for pitching, you are making it easier to send more pitches and therefore increase your odds of securing more work.

When writing your pitch, accurately portray your experience in the most favorable, but truthful way possible. Don't be afraid to share some of your awesome personality and humanize yourself.

Make sure to personalize your pitch when you have the right information and do a little research on the company you're applying to. Lastly, follow the directions listed exactly. Don't throw yourself out of the running before the competition actually starts.

Start by drafting a sample pitch email and selecting how many pitches to send per day or per week. Next, make sure to check your lead sources on a regular basis and submit your pitches as close to when the job ad comes out as possible. Lastly, don't forget to follow up with warm leads from time to time. You never know when it will pay off.

ACTION STEPS

1. Using the above templates as inspiration, draft your own pitch today. Remember, there's no need to be perfect. You *will* change it over time based on your samples and the feedback you receive from sending it out.

2. If you've been writing (via blogging for the web or in a different format), find a way to accurately portray your experience. Highlighting this will beef up your pitch, especially if you don't have any other samples yet.

3. Make sure to add a little of your personality to your pitch or include a personal detail or two to humanize yourself and your application.

4. Practice personalizing your next pitch by taking an extra minute or two to investigate your new potential employer's website or social media presence.

5. Make sure you read the next job listing that you intend to apply for extra carefully. Double check your pitch to make sure it meets the exact criteria required before hitting send.

6. Finalize your current pitch and save a copy of it as a draft in your email, so it's ready to go when you need it. Copy and paste to apply for future writing gigs.

7. Start tracking how many jobs you pitch versus how many you win. Based on the amount of clients you need, pick a number of pitches to submit per day or per week.

8. Try to check on your lead sources daily and pitch new listings ASAP.

9. Start an "Awaiting Reply" email folder to file initial job pitch responses in. Don't forget to follow up with existing leads over time.

Once you've sent out enough pitches, you'll start receiving inquiries from potential clients. This can be an exciting time. But you might be asking yourself, what now? Do I need a contract? How much should I charge? In the next chapter, I cover these important questions and more.

CHAPTER 8

Step Six: Land Your First Client

Gina Horkey

It's time to talk about what happens once you have a prospect interested in hiring you.

One of the first things a prospect is likely to ask you is, "What do you charge?" Imagine sending out tons of pitches, samples at the ready, and getting a one sentence reply like this. What do you say?

You don't want to bid too high in fear of scaring them off. But you don't want to bid too low and end up resenting the work because it doesn't pay well. So, how do you know what to charge?

FREELANCE WRITING RATES

If you Google how much freelance writers get paid or how to set your rate, you'll get varied and, in many cases, generic advice.

The rule of thumb is that the more specialized the niche, the higher the pay. This isn't a hard and fast rule, mind you. You can find clients in every niche looking to pay well in return for quality work. You can also find clients in every niche that are looking to pay as little as possible and still expect value.

This last group of clients are the worst. You don't want them.

From my experience and research over the past few years, I've concluded that a starting rate of $.10 per word is respectable. That means for a 500-word piece you'd be earning $50. And $100 for a 1,000-word piece.

Now, you might not start out at $.10 per word—I didn't. One of my first clients paid me $7.50 per 150- to 200-word WordPress theme review (if you know me at all, you'll probably laugh as I'm not the most "tech-savvy" individual, but it didn't prevent me from pursuing the work). The math equates to more like $.04 to .05 per word.

Not great, but not the worst I've ever heard of either. Another thing to keep in mind is that I was hired as a subcontractor for this gig. My client had actually been hired by the WP theme client and probably charged him closer to $.10 per word, netting the difference as his profit.

I was green, I needed the experience, and paying work is hands down better than working for free. But I didn't stay there long. After my feet were wet (or soaked, maybe?) I upped my rates to $.10 per word or a minimum of $50 per article and kept raising it from there.

My most recent personal finance piece (my primary niche) paid $553 for 700 to 900 words. *Five hundred and fifty-three dollars!* Crazy, right?

There are clients willing to pay well, but you might not be able to command those rates right off the bat. One of the reasons "niching down" is so powerful is that you can become an authority in that space and start charging premium rates.

Don't be afraid to start on the low end, though, with the goal of hitting $.10 per word sooner rather than later. Then, when you get there, shoot for $.15, then $.20 and go as high as your niche will allow.

Want to know something crazy? The better paying clients are usually the most pleasant to work with. It's counter-intuitive, but true. Your most challenging clients are also likely to be the ones that try to nickel and dime you. Beware!

PER WORD, PER HOUR, OR PER ARTICLE?

So far, we've been talking about charging per word. There are additional ways to calculate your fees, namely per hour or per article (per piece).

The favored advice at the moment is to either charge per word or per article, not per hour. If you're an efficient writer, then you don't want to worry about making less money because you write fast. Plus, I don't really care to track my time, especially if I get interrupted or pause an article. If I charge per word or per piece, I don't have to.

Most articles and blog posts range from 500 to 1,000 words. I used to quote a range of $.10 to .30 per word. This lets potential clients know that I'm a serious writer and jives with the above advice. For a 500-word piece, I wouldn't take less than $50.

The reason for the range was that if an assignment was easy for me to write and didn't take much additional research, then I was fine with a lower fee. Likely, it wouldn't take as much time and I'd make decent money.

There were times I'd go below $.10 per word for larger pieces that were efficient for me to write. For example, I had one client who paid me $75 for a 1,300 word article. $75 is a decent rate and the piece usually took me an hour or less to write. So, I'd make more than $50 per hour writing.

NEGOTIATING

As I discussed above, quoting a range is a great way to start off negotiations with a prospect. Here are a few more tips to help you become a master negotiator.

NEGOTIATION TIP #1: BE CONFIDENT

If you come from Corporate America, it can be hard to break free of the "employer/employee" mentality. In that relationship, the employer is in the power position (or at least that's how it feels). But I'm here to tell you that in the world of freelancing, it doesn't work that way.

Or at least it shouldn't.

You need to understand (and adopt the mindset) that you get to choose which clients to work with just as much as a client gets to choose the freelancer they work with. It's a partnership, not a dictatorship. You're trading skills or services for pay.

They're *not* your boss, they're your client. And you're there to help them further their business. Get the partnership part now?

However, this doesn't mean that you're the one in control, either. It just means that there should be a mutual level of respect. Usually, you're both self-employed small business owners. You're doing business together. So the goal should be that you help each other succeed. One should not profit immensely while the other simply collects a small paycheck.

NEGOTIATION TIP #2: KNOW YOUR WORTH

One of the reasons that I suggest $.10 per word as a minimum rate (after you get your feet wet) is because working for less makes it *very* difficult to build a sustainable business.

You need to be able to make a living, pay for self-employment taxes, your own benefits, vacation time, sick time, and more. You can't do that if you're working for peanuts. And if you're working for peanuts, then you're perpetuating the myth that writers shouldn't be paid well. That's crap, because writing is a big part of marketing...and marketing is what sells a product.

Another reason for quoting a range is that it allows you to bid higher if you think you'll need to negotiate. You can then settle somewhere in the middle or even toward the lower end and your client will think they're getting a deal.

The next step is to stick to your guns. Don't let clients negotiate you down in fear that you'll lose the gig. If that's the case, say "pass" and spend the time prospecting for someone who is willing to pay you what you're worth.

NEGOTIATION TIP #3: IT'S EASIER TO ASK FOR MORE MONEY UP FRONT THAN IT IS TO ASK FOR A RAISE

It can be hard to settle on a fee with a client and then later ask for a raise because you bid too low in the first place.

That's why you need to use the first two tips to ask for a livable wage from the get-go. If you don't, you're shooting yourself in the foot. Trust me, it's easy to get resentful if you're working for less than you should.

But whose fault is that, anyway? Yours! You're the one who agreed to a less-than-ideal wage, probably because you wanted to get the client. Again, risk walking away rather than agreeing to a low rate. You'll thank yourself later.

There will be a time when you'll move on from clients. Most likely it'll be because you've grown as a writer, both in confidence and skill, and you're ready to command more for your services.

When this happens, go to your client first and ask if they're able to meet your increased fee. If they're not, finish out your current cycle with them, thank them and be on your way. If they *are* willing to increase your rate, thank them and over-deliver on your next few pieces.

CONTRACTS

Now that you've pitched your prospect and they've agreed to your rate, what do you do? You want to get a contract in place.

I know, I know, contracts are awkward. Especially when you're just starting out.

Ironically, you don't usually enter into the conversation about contracts with a prospect until right when you start to feel like you're hitting it off. They're kind of a buzz kill that way.

While bringing up the subject of contracts with a new client will seem intimidating at first, once you've handled a few of these conversations you'll realize it's not that big of a deal. After all, contracts are a common part of the freelancing world. Almost everyone you write for will ask you to sign one and formally agree to their terms.

In our world, you're only likely to see two types of contracts. The most common one you'll see is a standard Writer's Agreement. The second is called a Non-Disclosure Agreement.

NON-DISCLOSURE AGREEMENTS (NDA)

Not all clients will ask you to sign these. But requests for them happen frequently enough to warrant a chat about what they are.

Essentially, an NDA is a document drafted by an attorney asking that you not talk about your interactions with a client with anyone who doesn't work directly for them. They can often get detailed about what you are allowed to say. You could potentially find yourself sued for something as small as revealing your boss's birthday to a friend.

WHO TYPICALLY ASKS FOR NDAS?

In theory, anyone could ask you to sign an NDA. But here are a few gigs in which you'll be more likely to do so.
> Ghostwriting gigs
> Working with successful authors
> Writing for major corporations
> Some magazines
> The Federal Government

If you have reservations about signing one, I completely understand. No one will fault you for opting out of signing an NDA. Unfortunately, however, it could cost you the job and relationship with your prospect.

WRITERS' AGREEMENTS (CONTRACTS)

Whatever you decide to call it, this is the document that lays out the terms under which you'll write for your client or prospect. It explains the details of your business relationship and you'll almost always receive one of these from an interested client, or provide one yourself.

Just like with the NDA, read through it carefully. Make sure you understand exactly what you're signing and that you agree to all the terms. Sometimes these documents will include an NDA in a section of the contract. It's their way of being more efficient by knocking out two birds with one 10-page stone. This works in their favor because if you don't agree to the NDA portion, you don't agree with the contract as a whole. However, you can always challenge or question individual clauses in a contract.

If you have questions, ask your client. If their answers don't help or if you're feeling more confused than you were before, get in touch with an attorney and ask him or her to explain it.

Including other jargon, you'll also notice a section within the contract that outlines your rate per word or per piece of X many words. Invoicing terms should be clear. You should have clear contact information for the person (or department) charged with issuing payments, the way you can expect to receive payments, and how long it'll take to make that happen once you send in your invoice.

Contracts can get wordy sometimes, depending on the client. Often, your client is in a hurry to cover a deadline, and you're in a hurry to land the gig. You get to work on your assignment, and hand it in along with your invoice. Did you just miss out on the only form of legal protection you had available to you?

If you and your new client forget to sign one, is it really that bad?

DO YOU REALLY NEED A CONTRACT?

I'm not going to lie. I haven't had a formal agreement in place with 75 percent of my clients. It's bad, I know. Especially since I'm about to give you the advice that you should.

Why should you?

Because you need to have certain details outlined in writing, whether they're part of a formally written and signed contract or informally in email conversations.

You read that right. Your email messages reflecting you and your client's agreed upon terms count—according to my business attorney friend, Karen Taggart.

Despite not having formal agreements with all of my clients and staff, I have been diligent about taking notes, making sure that we hammer out expectations on both sides and are clear about what we agree on by email. And I steer clear of prospects throwing up red flags.

Over time, you'll learn to recognize a bad client. Some examples of a red flag are prospects who are slow to respond, have vague requirements, or who try to negotiate your rate down. I also recommend ditching clients who expect you to be available 24/7 or who try to micro-manage your work. You're a professional freelancer and not a full-time employee.

CONTRACTS TRUMP ALL

You can't really prepare yourself for collection, because no one ever thinks they'll end up in that situation. Unfortunately, it does happen. And your agreement, either email correspondence clearly outlining your agreed upon terms or a formal contract, will help you collect what you're owed.

It almost happened to me once. I was hired to write regularly scheduled blog posts for a startup. Their "marketing plan changed" not two months after we got started working together, and they were my largest client at the time. All of this while I was preparing to leave my day job behind.

Suddenly, I had a hard time getting hold of them. And they still owed me $650 from my last invoice.

But we had a contract. #ContractForTheWin!

I was prepared to use one of my girlfriends (also an attorney) to enforce it. But luckily a direct phone call, which he actually answered, did the trick and funds were wired immediately.

I decided to get out while I could and not follow the 30 days' notice specified in the contract. Since I had trouble getting paid on what I had recently delivered, there was no way I was about to write another month's worth of content and fight for payment.

So, I just let it go. (Let it go, let it go...)

No extra work on my behalf and no payment needed on their end. Sometimes that makes the most sense.

Charging appropriate rates is essential to staying in business long-term. At a minimum, shoot for $.10 per word within the first six months or so. Then increase it from there as high as your niche will allow.

I also suggest that you price your services per word or per article, *not* per hour. Having a range to offer clients when they ask is nice, because then you can negotiate from there. If the project is research intensive, then you know to charge more. If it's easy or fun to do, then you can charge less.

Remember to be confident, know your worth, start high and don't compromise.

And when you're just getting started, it's okay to take on projects below your minimum to get samples. I certainly did! After you've built up sufficient samples, though, make sure that you assess each new project against your minimum fee.

Once you've gotten a client to agree to your rates, it's time to get a contract in place. Technically, any oral or written communication can hold up in court, but written contracts trump all.

ACTION STEPS

1. Calculate your ideal rate range per word, based on your minimum fee and 500 to 1,000 average words per article.

2. Pen out a plan for raising your rates over the next six to 12 months.

3. Adopt the mentality that you get to choose to work with a client just as much as they get to choose to work with you.

4. At a bare minimum, make sure to flesh out expectations clearly before starting your working relationship, get your client's written approval, and keep all email

communication with each client stored in a separate email folder in your inbox labeled by name.

5. Start using a contract with all new clients.

Next up, Sally talks about how to make the most of your freelance writing gigs so that you can earn your first $1,000.

CHAPTER 9

Step Seven: Earn Your First $1,000

Sally Miller

You've secured your first client. Congratulations! Now, it's time to knock their socks off and win more work. It's possible to earn your first $1,000 from one employer. But more often than not, it takes several gigs and multiple clients.

Which is why this first job is so important. Impress your client and they may reward you with more work. You'll also end up with a valuable writing sample that you can use to attract additional clients.

A WORD ABOUT FEAR

At this point, you may be feeling uncertain. I discussed common fears in chapter two. You learned how to quash your initial fears and start pitching.

Now you have a client and you want to do a good job. This can trigger a new set of fears.

First, take a deep breath and know that your worries are normal. You won this assignment based on the quality of your past work. You can do this.

If you need to, revisit chapter two. Many of the fear busting methods apply to the writing phase. Create a bad first draft, take one step at a time, or turn to a writing community for support. All of these strategies can help you deliver sparkling content for your new client.

THE WRITING PROCESS

Whether you're an experienced writer or a newbie, it's worth revisiting the basics. These days, most writing is for the web. However, my tips apply to all types of writing.

Before you start writing, you want to get to know your client. Study their website, articles, and other published material. Get a feel for their tone and style.

Also ask whether they have a style sheet or writing guidelines. Many blog owners expect you to include links to their previous articles, follow certain grammar rules, and more. Make sure you know your client's requirements.

Second, become familiar with the audience you're writing for. Are you targeting parents, teachers, scientists, academics? Different audiences call for different writing styles. Unless you're writing for academics, a good rule of thumb is to keep your writing at sixth grade reading level.

This may surprise you. Some people believe that good writing is complex. The opposite is true.

Clear and simple writing is always best. Most word processors, such as Microsoft Word, have built-in tools that assess the reading level of your work. You can also use an online tool such as Readability-Score.com.

Once you're familiar with your client and your audience, make sure you have a clear goal. What benefit does the reader get from reading your piece? Clients love it when you ask them questions like:

> Who is your target reader?
> What is the objective of this piece?
> What do you want your readers to get from reading this article?

These kinds of questions show that you're a professional who knows how to write for a specific audience.

Once you have all of this information, but not before, you're ready to begin writing. Everyone's writing process is different. This is what mine looks like...

First, I create an outline. I use mind mapping to get all of my ideas on paper. A mind map has a bubble in the center of the page. Around the bubble, I write all of my ideas. Once I have everything down, I organize my thoughts into a logical sequence. This is my outline.

Next, I sit down to write. I usually write the entire piece, which can be anything from 500 to 5,000 words, in one session. I write fast and don't edit as I go. I don't stop to look something up or do additional research. If I need a quote or reference, I leave a marker in the text and return to it later.

My goal at this stage is to get the words down quickly. The result isn't always pretty. I often cringe when I re-read my first draft. But that doesn't matter, because the next step fixes any problems.

I usually spend more time refining a piece than I do writing the first draft. During the self-editing phase, I complete research, check grammar, and review for readability. Below is an overview of my full self-editing process. You're welcome to copy this and adapt it for your own writing process.

MY SELF-EDITING PROCESS

When editing my own work, I hold a picture of my reader in my mind. This is a real person who represents my target audience. I then review my writing twice.

The first review is to make sure the piece achieves its goal. I ask myself:

1. Is each sentence clear, complete, and concise? I eliminate unnecessary words, including "really," "very," or just about any adverb.

2. Does each paragraph make one point? Are there relevant examples or evidence?

3. Does the introduction make a big promise? Does the conclusion leave the reader satisfied?

4. Does the entire piece have a logical sequence that achieves the end goal? Does each paragraph flow easily into the next?

The second review is to read the piece out loud. I listen to the rhythm, tweak words to improve readability, and correct any spelling or grammatical errors.

ARTICLE STRUCTURE

Something else that can help you write quickly, especially if you're struggling to create an outline, is to follow a template. As an example, here's a template I use for a standard blog post. Again, feel free to adapt this for your own use.

1. In the first few sentences, tell the reader what's in it for them. Also make your reader feel safe. You can do this by offering a roadmap, building a connection, or showing vulnerability.

2. Next, include three or four subheadings. Each subheading should have one main idea that is compelling to your reader. For example, be controversial, share an

emotional story, rile up the reader, or counter an objection. Back up your ideas with statistics, expert references, testimonials, or case studies.

3. In your conclusion, restate the hook or promise. If appropriate, include a call to action. Examples of a call to action include: subscribe to an email list, leave a comment, or share this article.

Not every article needs to, or should, be structured the same. But when you're new to freelancing, it's useful to start with a template that's proven to work.

You can use the above structure or study successful blogs. Then create your own templates based on the layouts they use.

MORE ABOUT WRITING CONVENTIONS

Earlier, I suggested you ask your client if they have a style sheet. Regardless of whether your client provides guidelines, it's a good idea to get to know writing conventions.

When I get stuck on a style point, I reference the AP Stylebook or The Yahoo Style guide. AP is best for journalistic writing and Yahoo for online writing.

There are many other style guides, all preferred in one field or another. For example, the Chicago Manual Style is favored for books and journals.

Style guides explain how to cite a source, use proper grammar, capitalize, and more. I find they're good for back-up, especially when I'm doubting myself. Plus, if you want to be professional, then you have to learn the basics.

Having said that, don't get too hung up on correct form. Grammar rules are constantly changing and even the popular style guides don't agree on every point.

Here're some of the most common conventions to give you an idea:

> Don't use all caps, bold, italics (with limited exceptions) or underlining (unless it's a link).

> Refer to books in italics instead of using quotes.

> Use a hyphen to create compound words. For example: "sugar-free."

> Punctuation should always be inside a quote. For example: "I love it!" Sarah replied.

> When writing for the web, be conversational and personable. But also authoritative.

And here's a checklist to help you write clear and compelling articles:

> Use sub-headings, bullets, bold, and white space to make your work easy to scan.

> Avoid big blocks of text. Keep paragraphs to one main idea and no more than three or four sentences.

> Keep sentences short. Consider breaking up compound sentences into two short sentences.

> One sentence paragraphs make an impact. Don't be scared to use them.

> Avoid meaningless words and sales speak. Some common offenders are: market-leading, world-class, breakthrough, utilize, alleviate, ultimate. These words are unimaginative and can be off-putting to the reader.

I've covered the basics so that you can confidently tackle your first writing gigs. If you want to further improve your writing, there are many online resources and books you can read. Some of my favorite books are:

> On Writing by Stephen King
> The War of Art by Steven Pressfield
> Bird by Bird by Anne Lamott
> The Elements of Style by William Strunk Jr. and E. B. White
> On Writing Well by William Zinsser

Again, don't let perfection be your enemy. It's good to learn from more experienced writers. But you can absolutely get started as a freelance writer, regardless of your current level of experience.

HEADLINES THAT WOW

There's one last challenge that many writers struggle with. And that's crafting a headline.

I typically write the headline (if required) last. You may not need to write the headline. Or you may be asked to come up with two or three options.

When you have to create a headline, follow these rules:

1. Keep your headline short. Eight words or less if possible.

2. Be specific. Include numbers to quantify results where appropriate.

3. Offer the reader a reason to read the article. This may be a benefit, an answer to a burning question, or a solution to a big problem.

4. Consider whether you can add intrigue to your headline. This isn't necessary but it's a useful strategy.

I'm a fan of templates because they're a great way to streamline your writing process. I've already shared a basic template for writing a blog post. I also use templates to come up with headline ideas. Below are some sample templates to help you get started.

HEADLINE TEMPLATE #1: CURIOSITY

The Surprising Truth About [Topic]
The [Subject Area] Tricks Being Used On You
Do You Make These 3 [Subject Area] Mistakes?
5 Surprising Reasons Why [Topic]

HEADLINE TEMPLATE #2: BENEFIT OR SOLUTION TO AN URGENT PROBLEM

How to Achieve [Benefit] Without [Something Tedious]
How to Master [Problem] In [Time Period]
The Secret to [Benefit]
Get Rid of [Problem] Once And For All

HEADLINE TEMPLATE #3: FEAR

5 Reasons Why [Fear] And What You Can Do About It
What Never to Do In [Your Industry Or Sub-Industry]
Warning: [Thing Not to Do]
The Shocking Truth About [Topic]

HEADLINE TEMPLATE #4: CONTROVERSY

Why [Common Belief] Is Not True
Why You Should Stop Doing [Something Everyone Is Doing]
The Case Against [Something Everyone Is Doing]
Why You Don't Need [Something Everyone Else Says You Need]

HEADLINE TEMPLATE #5: LISTS AND NUMBERS

10 Ways to Do [Something Your Audience Cares About]
The 7 Rules of [Your Topic]
3 Hacks to Do [Something] That Work Every Time
5 Things Your [Trusted Person] Won't Tell You

DELIVERING YOUR ASSIGNMENT AND GETTING PAID

You've researched and written your piece. There's one more thing to do—deliver your finished assignment.

This last point is obvious, but I'll make it anyway. Don't miss any deadlines and be sure to get paid for your work.

Send your finished piece to your client on time and in the format requested. Some clients accept a Microsoft Word or Google document. Others ask you to post directly to their WordPress blog.

Once you deliver your assignment, expect to make revisions. Do the requested changes and don't take feedback personally. It takes time for a writer and client to get to know each other. Revisions are part of the process.

Last of all, don't forget to get paid! How and when you're paid should be defined in your contract (Gina covered this in the previous chapter). I usually send my client an invoice when I deliver the completed piece. For larger projects, such as a case study or white paper, I ask for half the payment upfront. If you have a regular client, you can also agree on a monthly retainer.

ACTION STEPS

1. Once you have an assignment, get to know the audience and goal of the piece you're going to write.

2. Familiarize yourself with your client's conventions (if any) or reference a style guide as needed.

3. Research and write your piece. If you want feedback, share in a community and ask for a critique.

4. Deliver your assignment and get paid.

5. Use your piece to get more work and earn your first $1,000. I'll talk more about how to do this in the final chapter.

That's it—you now have everything you need to land your first client(s) and make money as a freelance writer. In the last chapter, I cover the basic business questions so that you can start earning money straight away.

CHAPTER 10

It's Time To Begin

Sally Miller

That moment you receive your first paycheck is magical. You feel amazing. You're finally earning money doing something you love. You're a paid writer.

So, what now?

If you haven't taken action yet, start today. We've given you everything you need to start your freelance writing business.

If you're worrying about accounting, taxes, and business structure, then stop. You don't have to handle all of these things before you begin.

I can't tell you how often I hear questions such as:

> *Do I need to incorporate?*
> *How do I file taxes?*
> *Do I need to fill out government forms?*

Here's the thing: these are the *least* important questions to be asking. Seriously, don't let red tape stop you from achieving your dreams.

I'm not saying that you can skip these steps. You can't. But more often than not, these questions are excuses. They are reasons not to start, and they are caused by your fear.

According to the Freelancers Union, there are nearly 54 million freelancers in the U.S. There are many more millions in countries like the U.K., Australia, and India.

If all of these people can figure it out, then so can you.

However, I'm not going to leave your questions unanswered. As a perfectionist who seeks answers to every question, I get it. In this chapter, I'll address all of your business and legal concerns so that you have no more reasons to delay your freelancing career.

WHAT BUSINESS STRUCTURE DO YOU NEED?

Here in the U.S., it's easy to get started as a freelancer. You don't need to formally create a business, unless you want to.

I started out as a sole proprietor. A sole proprietorship is an unincorporated business with one owner. You pay personal income tax on profits from the business. I also operate under my own name, so don't need a DBA.

DBA is an abbreviation for "doing business as." For example, if you decide to call your business "Speedy Writing Services," then you need to file a DBA to use that name. Registering your DBA is done with either your county clerk's office or your state government, depending on where your business is located.

The main downside of a sole proprietorship is that you're personally liable. You need to personally cover any debts, losses, or lawsuits that can't be paid by your business.

I still operate as a sole proprietor and I'm comfortable doing so. Gina, on the other hand, has a more complex business. She sells coaching, courses, virtual assistance services, and more. Gina operates her business as an S Corporation (S Corp).

An S Corp is a U.S. business structure that allows you to avoid double taxation (once to the corporation and again to the shareholders). It's similar to a Limited Liability Company (LLC). Both are typically pass-through entities, meaning that business profit or loss is passed-through to your personal tax return. They also offer limited liability protection. You cannot be held personally liable for the company's debts or liabilities.

The best business structure for you is going to depend on your circumstances. Do your research, consult a lawyer, or ask a local business advisory group.

If you decide to form an LLC or S Corp, you can quickly set one up using a service like Legal Zoom. For a fee, they fill out all the paperwork for you. I did this for my first business (which had nothing to do with freelance writing and was structured as an LLC).

If you live outside of the U.S., then check your local options. It's easy to do. Ask a local freelance group, contact a lawyer, or search your government's website. There's no shortage of advice on how to start a business.

Don't let this small step hold you back from following your dreams. Also remember that you can always start out with the simplest business structure and change things later.

ACCOUNTING FOR YOUR BUSINESS

Besides legal, there are some financial considerations. You want to figure out how to handle bookkeeping and pay taxes. Unless you live in a tax-free haven, you'll need to pay taxes on your income.

I keep my business finances separate from my personal finances. I do this by using a separate business account. I also have a PayPal account that I use only for business purposes. Many people who hire freelancers are most comfortable using PayPal.

It took 30 minutes at my local bank to set up my business account. The account is free, though I have to keep a minimum balance to avoid charges. Your current bank will be happy to explain their business offerings. Or you can shop around for a free account that meets your needs.

If you want to keep things simple, you can start out with just a PayPal account. I recommend getting a business PayPal account. If you're already a PayPal user, it's easy to upgrade from a personal account to a business account. Otherwise, visit PayPal's website and select the business option from the menu.

PayPal's business account includes several perks, such as better reporting and the ability to send invoices to your clients. It's free to set up. PayPal makes money by charging you a fee every time you receive a payment.

Remember to use your dedicated account(s) for all business related income and expenses. This makes keeping detailed records much easier. Which brings us to the next topic...bookkeeping.

Now, don't be put off by the idea of bookkeeping. It doesn't have to be complex.

Bookkeeping is simply the act of recording every transaction for your business. You want to know who paid you, when they paid you, how much they paid you, and what they paid you for (and the same for expenses).

Keep your books up to date and tax time will be a breeze. We'll get to taxes in a moment. First, let's look at exactly what you need to track and how to do it.

I record all income and expenses in a spreadsheet. I created my own, based on one Gina shares in her Freelance Writing Course. It has a tab for each month of the year. The front page is a rolling total and has an entry for each month.

Your income is what you get paid for your freelance services. Your expenses are what you pay out to support your writing business.

I document any income received (not invoiced, but actually received in the bank) and any business expenses I've incurred in the corresponding month's tab. It's like a budget for my business in present tense, or what's happening now.

Some examples of business expenses are:
> Office supplies
> Telephone and Internet service
> Books, magazines, reference materials
> Membership in professional organizations
> Equipment such as a laptop you use for your business
> Legal and professional fees

Make sure you keep all receipts. I have a folder on my laptop for any electronic receipts and an envelope for physical receipts.

I do my bookkeeping once a month. The process is simple and takes less than 30 minutes. I open up my business bank account and copy over every transaction for the prior month into my bookkeeping spreadsheet. I also make sure I write a brief description of each transaction and have a corresponding receipt on file.

PAYING TAXES

Nobody likes paying taxes, but it's a necessary step.

If you follow my advice and keep records, then taxes are easy. You can either give your bookkeeping spreadsheet to your tax advisor or fill out the required forms yourself.

It's a good idea to start setting aside a portion of your business income to plan for future taxes. You're going to owe taxes on your new income stream, and you have to pay both the employer and employee tax portions when you're self-employed in the U.S. I recommend setting aside 20 to 30 percent of your net income.

I use the term net income because your business expenses serve as a tax deduction. Different expenses are deducted differently (for example, office rent versus client meals), so bear in mind that it's not a straight dollar for dollar offset.

Feel free to consult with your accountant. I'm not a tax advisor and all of our situations are different.

One final note on U.S. taxes. Freelancers typically pay taxes every quarter. However, in your first year you probably won't need to do this. As you grow your business, be aware of when you need to start paying quarterly instead of annually. Otherwise you may be hit with penalties and interest.

As I'm U.S. based, this is obviously from a U.S. tax perspective. If you live outside of the U.S., do your research and plan according to your governing tax laws.

BEYOND YOUR FIRST CLIENT

Before I close, I want to return to an important topic. At the end of the last chapter, I mentioned follow-up work. This is how you will quickly earn your first $1,000.

There are a few additional steps you want to take with every client (or at least the ones you like). Do these things and you will quickly win more writing gigs:

1. Ask for a testimonial. I prefer to wait for a suitable opportunity before doing this. If a client thanks me for my work, I'll use this as an opening to ask if they'd mind providing a testimonial. You want to make it easy for your client to say yes. One way to do this is to draft an example testimonial for them to edit and approve. Once you have a glowing write-up, don't forget to display it on your website.

2. Update your writing portfolio. Gina discussed your portfolio in chapter five. You will want to keep this fresh by displaying your best work. As you complete more freelance assignments, you'll get new samples. You can add these or even replace older ones. Make sure you keep a good mix that appeals to the type of client you want to work with.

3. Ask for more work. As with testimonials, pick a suitable time before pitching an existing client for more work. Always be on the lookout for opportunities. For example, if your client is releasing a new product or service, they may need new marketing materials. Most clients prefer to work with a freelancer they already know rather than hiring someone new. Don't be afraid to send an email offering to help them out.

YOUR TURN

Congratulations—you made it to the end! You now have everything you need to begin your freelance writing career. It's time to decide:

> *Are you ready to start earning money doing something you love?*
> *Do you want freedom from your nine-to-five?*
> *What would your life look like if you could work from anywhere and at any time?*

Follow the seven steps in this book and your dreams will become a reality. Gina and I have already shared how freelance writing has changed our lives for the better.

Now it's your turn. Start today and move one step closer to earning your first $1,000 as a freelance writer.

ABOUT SALLY MILLER

Sally is a mom on a mission. She is passionate about answering the question, "Can modern moms have it all?" In a previous life, Sally worked for nineteen years as a project manager and business analyst in London and Silicon Valley. She has a Bachelor's Degree in Computer Science and a Master's Degree in Business Administration.

When her daughter was born, she discovered a new purpose. Sally left her corporate career to be a stay-at-home mom. She wanted to be a full-time mom to her kids. However, she missed the freedom and purpose that came from working. So Sally made a decision: she'd find a way to stay home with her kids and earn an income (without feeling torn between the two).

Sally is a self-confessed research geek and compulsive planner. She loves learning how stuff works, mastering new skills, and sharing her knowledge with others. You can find out more by visiting her website: sallyannmiller.com.

ABOUT GINA HORKEY

Gina Horkey is a married, millennial mama to two precocious toddlers from Minnesota. Additionally, she's a professional writer and online business marketing consultant with a decade of experience in the financial services industry.

A psychology major by education, Gina left Corporate America behind at the end of 2014 after building a successful freelance writing and virtual assistant business on the side of her full-time job as a personal financial advisor. Her better half, Wade, left work behind the year before to become a stay-at-home dad to their two littles, and they've never regretted either life-changing decision since!

Online business has become Gina's newest passion and she enjoys helping other freelancers gear up to quit their day jobs and take their side hustles full-time via her website: horkeyhandbook.com. Stop by to follow her journey, enjoy some fabulous FREE resources, and peruse her monthly income reports.

Made in the USA
Middletown, DE
24 October 2018